STITCHING PATHWAYS

Successful Quilting on Your Home Machine

by Wendy Sheppard

Landauer Publishing, LLC

Stitching Pathways
Copyright © 2017 by Landauer Publishing, LLC
Projects Copyright © 2017
by Wendy Sheppard

This book was designed, produced,
and published by
Landauer Publishing, LLC
3100 100th Street, Urbandale, IA 50322
515/287/2144 800/557/2144 landauerpub.com

President/Publisher: Jeramy Lanigan Landauer
Editor/Art Director: Laurel Albright
Editor/Photographer: Sue Voegtlin

Landauer Books are distributed
to the Trade by
Fox Chapel Publishing
1970 Broad Street
East Petersburg, PA 17520
www.foxchapelpublishing.com
1-800-457-9112

For consumer orders:
Landauer Publishing, LLC
3100 100th Street
Urbandale, Iowa 50322
www.landauerpub.com
1-800-557-2144

Library of Congress Control Number: 2017955336

ISBN: 978-1-935726-93-7

This book printed on acid-free paper.
Printed in United States

10-9-8-7-6-5-4-3-2-1

TABLE OF CONTENTS

Introduction 4

Stitching Pathways & Techniques 5

Keys to Free-Motion Success 6

The Essentials & Beyond 9

My Favorite Tools and Threads 10

Layering and Basting the Quilt Top 17

Burying the Thread Tails 18

Importance of Doodling 19

One Way to Practice 20

Achieving Even Quilting 21

Determining What and Where to Quilt . . . 22

Quilting Negative Space 23

Quilting Appliqué Shapes 24

Allover Quilting 25

Quilting a Borderless Quilt 26

Straight Line Quilting 27

Stitch Variations 28

My Two Cents
INTRODUCTION

Hello Quilting Friends! I'm so glad you decided to check out my Stitching Pathways book! Stitching Pathways is, by far, the book that is the nearest and dearest to me.

When I started quilting 12 years ago, I was intrigued by the idea of quilting my own quilts on a domestic machine. I liked how the quilting changed the personality of a quilt depending on how it was quilted.

I was particularly attracted to feather quilting. It was the first quilting motif I set out to teach myself on my home machine after reading books by Harriet Hargrave and Diane Gaudynski. I was young and naive then. I thought my feather quilting looked pretty good on my fifth or sixth quilt. So I proceeded to enter one of them in a local quilt show. The only problem was, my quilt was all wonky, it didn't lay flat, and of course, it didn't do so well.

Over the years, domestic machine quilting has remained a passion in my quilting journey. I love designing and constructing quilt tops but I have always savored the quilting part. I have come to realize that constructing quilting tops brings out the engineer in me. I enjoy the challenge of accurately piecing the quilt blocks. But the artist in me comes out to play when a quilt is ready to be quilted.

Domestic machine quilting is one of the topics I share on my blog (www.wendysheppard.net). I started it about 10 years ago to document my journey as a quilter. I started a popular series called Thread Talk to specifically address the different aspects of domestic machine quilting. Whether talking about my favorite threads and batting, what works and doesn't work, or schematics of quilting motifs, quilters near and far tell me how my Thread Talk series has helped them in their own quilting journey.

Many have asked for a book compiling the Thread Talk posts on my blog. In the past, I have directed quilters to my online and DVD machine quilting classes, but quilters continue to ask for a book because they "don't want to get on the computer to find the information" or, "I just want a book that I can flip through for help." And at long last, here it is—the book!

So you can see how special this book is to me. It is essentially a book that tracks my own quilting journey. It is a book written by a quilting friend (Me!) to a quilting friend, (You!). I hope you enjoy your own exciting quilting journey when we explore the various "Stitching Pathways"!

Quiltingly yours,

STITCHING PATHWAYS

As I mentioned in the introduction, Stitching Pathways is written by me, your quilting friend. Through Stitching Pathways, I've tried to condense the tips and tricks I've learned in my years of quilting on my domestic machine.

I taught myself how to machine quilt feathers first, then I moved on to simpler motifs. I'm a firm believer that different quilters learn differently by taking different "pathways". Stitching Pathways is written so that it can be picked up and opened anywhere. It doesn't have to be read cover to cover. Simply find the topic that interests you at the moment and flip to the page to read up!

So what are you waiting for?

TECHNIQUES

Quilting motif possibilities are endless, and in Stitching Pathways, I'll share stitching schematics of some of my favorites. If you have followed my *Thread Talk* posts on my blog, schematics are the hand-drawn sketches that show where I start stitching and how I progress through the design with my stitches.

Once you've started at the beginning of a design, arrows will direct your stitching pathway. "Breathing and resting points" are indicated by dots with numbers. Take advantage of these places. Stopping and taking a breath will help you relax, regroup, and get ready for the next line of stitches.

The colors change in the diagram as you stitch. All starting points will be a solid line with arrows and dots. When you've completed the first section, the solid line becomes a dotted stitch line and the next section becomes a new color. A color legend will help you see your stitch progression throughout the motif.

KEYS TO FREE-MOTION SUCCESS

FREE-MOTION QUILTING AND TAKING THE PLUNGE

"Free-motion" is quilting with the feed dogs of your machine disengaged. **You can stitch forward, backward, or side-to-side and never have to turn your project.** Your hands become the tool that moves the quilt as you stitch. You can stitch freely in any direction using creative shapes to quilt your quilt. And it's easy to do on your home machine! Even when my quilting friends are hesitant, I always encourage them to jump in and give domestic machine quilting a try. Most of the time, quilting their own quilts creates a feeling of great satisfaction, too. Techniques, tips, and tricks fill the pages of this book to start you on your own path to machine quilting.

PRACTICE, PRACTICE, PRACTICE!

Practice makes perfect. The more you practice, the better your quilting will be. First, doodle on paper to see how the direction of each movement takes you along a path. Then, make several quilt sandwiches and practice with your home machine.

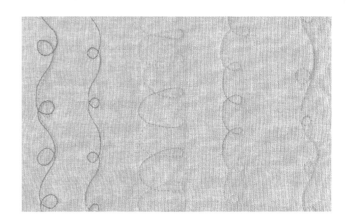

MUSCLE MEMORY AND MANEUVERING THE QUILT SANDWICH

One thing to be mindful of is that the feed dogs are disengaged when you're moving a quilt sandwich. With nothing to move it as you stitch, your hands, arms and muscles become the "feed dogs" and they have the job of maneuvering your quilt under the needle. Muscle memory refers to repeating a movement, over and over, until it becomes second nature. See how moving the sandwich and changing the speed of your machine will change your stitch length.

MY FAVORITE TOOLS AND NOTIONS

Like any kind of sewing or quilting, we find tools that work best to accomplish what we want to do. I'm sharing my favorites because they work for me and if you are unsure of what tools, thread, batting and other notions you need to start free-motion quilting, you can try my favorites to get started. I can't stress the importance of thread, batting and needle choice. Besides your machine, these notions may be the most important choices you make when you start out.

BUILD FROM THE BASICS

I like to start my students quilting echoes. Echoing is simply sewing around the edge of a shape and then stitching another line a small distance away from the first. It is the most basic motif in machine quilting that builds muscle memory, muscle control, and the ability to maneuver curves. I also teach my students to look at the needle and where it lands. Training your eyes in this way and not relying on the edges of a machine foot will help stitches land accurately. This is important as you begin to learn the basics.

IMPORTANCE OF DOODLING

I recommend that you doodle with a pencil or pen on paper before using your machine to quilt your design. It's great practice and you can visualize where to go next from one area to another. While doodling may seem like such a simple process, it helps you think about how a particular quilting path affects the next direction a stitch should take. When you feel comfortable doodling on paper, try it out on a practice sandwich.

PRACTICE SANDWICHES

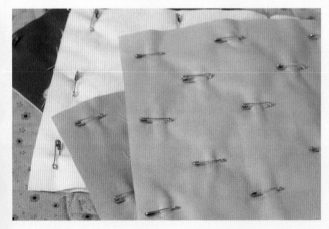

I suggest to my friends to first try out quilting motifs by making practice sandwiches. Sandwiches are a great way to test the scale of a motif, correct and experiment with thread tension, and movement. Use a light solid color fabric and contrasting thread so you can easily see your stitches. Make several sandwiches at a time to have on hand when you want to try a new technique. This is also a great way to use up scrap fabric and batting pieces you have saved.

Refer to page 17 to make a practice sandwich.

PANELS AND FOLLOWING THE LINES

I encourage beginning quilters to jump right into the quilting part by using printed panels. Time is saved just by layering the quilt sandwich and getting right to the business of quilting! Quilt panels that have motifs and designs already printed on them make it easy to practice follow-the-line quilting. Stitch slowly. This will help you see where to go next, and reduces the chance of snags and jerks, which improves overall stitch quality.

My Two Cents on Technical Stuff
THE ESSENTIALS & BEYOND

Resources abound that cover the essentials of domestic machine quilting. It is not my intention to write another book that covers the same topics these resources do, but to share with you how I went from not knowing how to sew to being able to quilt anything I wanted with beautiful results! In this chapter, I explain some of what has worked for me, what some of my trusted notions are, and how these methods and tools contribute to stunning results.

My Favorite Tools and Threads

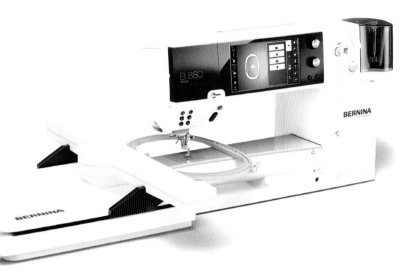

For me, Domestic Machine Quilting consists of two machine techniques:

1. Feed Dogs are engaged when using a walking foot to quilt straight lines or piecing.

2. Feed dogs are disengaged when a quilting foot is used. The quilter becomes the "feed dogs" by maneuvering the quilt sandwich under the needle. Quilting done in this manner is generally referred to as free-motion quilting.

WALKING FOOT

This foot allows all layers of a quilt sandwich to move through the machine evenly as you stitch. Some of today's machines have a built-in walking foot while it is an added accessory on other machines.

FREE-MOTION OR DARNING FOOT

In addition to the walking foot, the main presser foot used in machine quilting is the free-motion foot. It is also referred to as a darning foot. A free-motion foot made of clear plastic allows better visibility when stitching. If you do not own one, it is well worth the investment. Check with your dealer to purchase one compatible with the type and model of your sewing machine.

FEED DOGS

Feed dogs are raised (photo 1) for piecing, but should be lowered (photo 2) when free-motion stitching. This allows you to move your quilt smoothly under the needle.

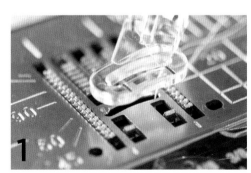

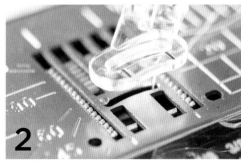

SEWING MACHINE TENSION

Movement and machine speed are important in perfecting your quilt stitches. But if your sewing machine tension is not set right, those perfect stitches become not-so-perfect!

Machine stitches should look the same on both sides of your quilt. They should be evenly spaced and lie flat against the fabric. The stitches should lock somewhere within the batting of your quilt sandwich.

If you see bobbin thread coming to the top of your quilt, the tension is too tight. To correct, lower the number on your top tension dial in very small increments.

If dots of thread appear on the back of your quilt, the top tension is too loose. Move the tension dial to a higher number to tighten the tension.

Always do some test stitching as you make small changes in your tension, and don't hesitate to refer to your machine manual for additional help.

TIP

One common frustration in free-motion quilting is when a bunch of tangled thread (called "bird nests") shows-up on the back of the quilt. Genie Magic Bobbin Washers eliminate backlash when changing quilting direction at high speeds. They fit in all domestic machine bobbins.

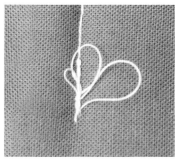

Thread Talk
FROM MY SEWING MACHINE

2¢ My Two Cents

A common question I'm asked is whether a stitch regulator is a must. For me it is, and I wish every domestic machine came with one. I learned to free-motion quilt with Bernina's BSR. It produces neat, consistent stitches of the same length while quilting and it reacts to the movement of fabric and adjusts to the speed of the machine automatically. But a stitch regulator isn't necessary for successful machine quilting. Check with the manufacturer to see if there is an after-market regulator available for your machine.

I've taught students who quilt better without a regulator. Always experiment before purchasing a machine. Some dealers offer quilting classes that let you use their machines. Take advantage of those classes to determine the machine you prefer.

Thread Talk

FROM MY SEWING MACHINE

 My Two Cents

An interesting snippet on the construction of the Royal wedding gown worn by the Duchess of Cambridge:

"The RSN worked closely with the Alexander McQueen atelier team. The hand-stitchers washed their hands every thirty minutes to keep the lace and threads pristine, and changed the needles every three hours to keep them sharp."

The point is – changing out your needles frequently ensures quality.

NEEDLES

Machine needles come in many sizes and are made for different uses and thread weights. Usually, you will see two numbers on a needle packet listed like this: 90/14. The smaller number is the American sizing system and the smaller the number the finer the needles.

I use either Microtex (Sharp) or Quilting needles, generally 90/14 on my Bernina machines when quilting with cotton threads. It seems large but with this size, I find that I have fewer skipped stitches, particularly when quilting over bulky seams. Finer threads, such as silk, require a smaller needle like a 70/10 size.

I intuitively like to use Microtex Sharp needles because they have a very thin, sharp point and a narrow shaft. They are perfect for detailed stitching when free-motion quilting.

I change my needle once every project, sometimes more often, if I'm quilting an important piece for a quilt show. If you notice that your stitches are not looking quite as nice and tight as you expect them to be, chances are you need to change your needle.

> **TIP**
>
> *Not long after I learned to sew, I heard this nifty tip that I still use today to dispose of used needles. Use an empty medicine bottle to dispose of your old needles. If you have children in your home, it will keep them safe with the childproof cap and the person who removes the trash won't get pricked. I still have my original medicine bottle — it is surprising the number of needles it holds.*

THREAD

I love threads more than I love fabrics! When I first started quilting I used 100 weight silk thread because it was so fine that it masked my mistakes. Then I discovered Aurifil 50 weight cotton thread. It does the same for me as silk threads, and it is cotton! Now it is my go-to thread for piecing, appliqué and machine quilting and a staple in my thread box.

I always recommend first time machine quilters try Aurifil 50 weight thread. When it is used tone-on-tone with fabric, it is fine enough to mask uneven movements or mistakes a beginner will probably experience. And because the thread is so fine, I can quilt multiple passes along the same path without visible thread buildup.

Aurifil threads are noted for their lack of lint, which is another feature I like. This means I can quilt for a long time before I have to clean out the bobbin area of my machine.

I know many quilters who try to match the bobbin thread to the color of the backing fabric. But I always match my top and bobbin thread. There are times, even with my machine set just right, the bobbin thread will show up on my quilt top. If the bobbin color is different from the top thread color, my quilting might become unsightly and I have to rip out stitches. I save myself from this frustration by matching top and bobbin threads. And sometimes, I get very pretty and unexpected visual results when my bobbin thread ends up contrasting with the backing fabric color.

I love Aurifil thread but experimenting with new types, weights, and colors can be fun and change the look of your machine quilting altogether. The weight of thread differs from one thread manufacturer to another. Threads that work well in my machine may not work as well in yours. Use your best judgment in determining what thread to use.

2¢ My Two Cents

TIP

Once you become comfortable with machine quilting, you might want to try using different thread weights to see how it affects your stitching. The smaller the number indicating weight, the heavier the thread becomes. When I experimented with Aurifil 40 weight, I found it showed the quilting a little better. I would choose this weight for a wholecloth quilt to show strong contrast. Aurifil 28 weight definitely showcases my quilting more prominently, but because it's heavier, thread build-up made from stitching over previously stitched paths quickly becomes more noticeable.

Thread Talk
FROM MY SEWING MACHINE

2¢ My Two Cents

CONTRAST THREAD

As you are learning and improving, you may want to use a subtly contrasting thread, such as this pink on white color scheme. You can see the quilting better with the subtle contrast in color than you can if your thread matches the fabric perfectly, but it is more forgiving of small mistakes than a high contrast thread color. I almost always quilt with a subtle contrast color scheme now because I really love how a slightly different color of thread adds to the quilting. Plus, you get to use fun colors other than beige and white.

CHOOSING THREAD COLOR

As a beginner, and on a practice sandwich, you will want to use a thread color that contrasts with your fabric so you can see your stitches and what you need to improve on. I always suggest practicing on a small practice sandwich as you are learning. Using a contrasting thread on a light background will visually magnify any little hiccups or mistakes. When you are ready to quilt on your quilt, you will likely want to use a matching or subtly contrasting thread.

TIP

IF YOU WANT TO USE A CONTRASTING THREAD ON YOUR QUILT...

Be very familiar with the flow of the pattern that you want to quilt, especially if the pattern is being free-handed. Any jerky stops or pauses will show much more with a contrasting thread versus a matching thread. Practicing and knowing the flow of your quilting pattern will definitely minimize that problem.

BATTING

SILK

I like Hobbs silk batting because it is light and airy, making my quilt sandwich less bulky and heavy. It makes it easier to move it around under the throat area of my sewing machine, too. Unlike cotton batting, quilts using silk batting will maintain a soft feel and drape well when quilted heavily or densely. It has more loft than cotton so it will showcase your quilting very well.

Silk batting is washable, but with any batting you use, you will want to check out the laundry and care information included on the package and pre-shrink if necessary.

WOOL

The high loft of wool batting highlights feather quilting wonderfully when the background is quilted down with dense quilting.

Wool batting is what I use when quilting appliqué quilts. I generally only outline quilt around my appliqué shapes, and then heavily quilt down the rest of the quilt. That makes my appliqués pop and take on a trapunto effect.

Also, wool batting doesn't make a heavily quilted quilt feel like cardboard like cotton batting does. The quilt will maintain a soft feel and drapes well.

COTTON

My preference in cotton batting is Hobbs Tuscany bleached cotton batting. I use cotton batting when I quilt borderless quilts. Cotton batting tends to "stick" better to fabrics in the quilt sandwich. There is less distortion of the squareness of the quilt, especially when I am not able to trim the quilt when squaring it up, as is the case with many borderless quilts. I recommend using cotton batting for small projects like runners and tablemats as well.

Thread Talk
FROM MY SEWING MACHINE

2¢ My Two Cents

Before you decide which batting is right for your project, you might want to sample some different types and weights.

Make up a few practice sandwiches with the samples and see how your quilting looks.

Keep your samplers for reference and write down what kind of batting is used in each one.

Thread Talk

FROM MY SEWING MACHINE

My Two Cents

When I first started machine quilting, I used the Supreme Slider tool to help me overcome jerky movements and stitches.

The Supreme Slider is made of pure Teflon which makes my sewing surface very slick and increases the ease of moving my quilts when I am quilting. Using this tool, my quilt turns very nicely with any sort of curvy quilting. It comes in handy especially when I am handling a big quilt. I should mention that the Supreme Slider only works when your feed dogs are down. Check the manufacturer's website for the size that will best fit the bed of your machine.

The silicon back of the slider grips the machine bed nicely. It is easily washable with soap and water. After I have it in place, I add a little piece of tape for more security.

TOOLS

MARKERS

I use washable fabric markers on light fabrics, and white markers that are removable by high heat on dark fabrics.

MARKING

I am often asked whether I mark or don't mark my quilts for quilting. I base my decision on how I envision the end result of my quilting. I have marked heavily, sparsely, and none at all.

When I make wholecloth quilts, I definitely mark my design but only mark the main motif. The background, or negative space, is unmarked and free-handed.

Sometimes I let the piecing in the quilt guide my design for quilting. I may fill negative space around an appliqué with pebbles. Sometimes I quilt a motif entirely within a square. Because I generally do all my quilting without marking, I suggest again to practice, practice, practice on small quilt sandwiches. Gaining confidence in this way will come to life when you transfer those skills to your first quilt.

> ### TIP
>
> **HOUSEHOLD ITEMS:**
>
> Household items can be used to mark quilting lines and patterns. I use bowls, plates, bottle caps, etc., to get the shape and size I desire for certain patterns.

LAYERING AND BASTING THE QUILT TOP

Pin basting is my favorite method to hold my quilt sandwich together. I start by taping down the backing to a large flat surface, making sure it is wrinkle free. This also keeps puckering from happening during the quilting process. After layering and smoothing the batting, I lay the quilt top on the batting, making sure it's centered and flat. I pin the quilt sandwich every 1-1/2"-2" starting from the quilt center and working outward. I remove pins as I quilt, leaving a 6"-8" area free of pins. If at any time, I think a pin might get caught by the machine in the quilting area, I just go ahead and remove it.

MAKE A PRACTICE SANDWICH

Cut (2) 8-10" squares of light fabric and 1 square of batting to fit fabric squares. Layer batting between fabric squares and pin baste in place. Make several sandwiches to have on hand.

Leave a section in the center free of pins to start stitching. Use a contrasting thread to easily see your stitches and stitching path and remove pins as you continue to stitch.

2¢ My Two Cents

WHERE DO I START QUILTING?

I'm frequently asked whether I quilt from the center of the quilt outward. Ideally yes, and I do that whenever a quilt is manageable. If a quilt is just too large, I start from where it's convenient. I firmly believe that if a quilt is well basted, it doesn't matter where one starts quilting.

Thread Talk

2¢ My Two Cents

When I free-motion quilt, I use one hand to move the quilt and the other hand to slightly lift an edge. This gives my quilt a little "pick me up" and it tends not to get caught or drag, making it just a bit easier to move the quilt. I find that using the palm of both my hands actually impedes me from moving the quilt sandwich freely.

BURYING THE THREAD TAILS

When you start to machine quilt, you will need to know what to do with the thread tails as you start and finish. I always pull my bobbin thread up before I start. That way, I won't have a tail hanging of the back of my quilt to deal with.

With the presser foot down, take ahold of the top thread with your left hand and rotate the wheel to bring the needle down and up.

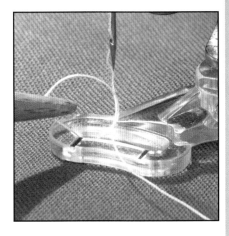

The bobbin thread should come up from the bottom as a loop, as shown. Grab the loop with a pin or stiletto and pull it through to the top.

To start quilting, take 4-5 very tiny stitches before moving on. Continue quilting and when you come to a stopping place, top and bottom threads are still on top. Take 4-5 tiny stitches to lock.

To bury the "tails", I run them through the eye of a needle, run the needle exactly into the starting/stopping point, then run the needle through the middle of the sandwich without going through to the back. Run the needle and thread several inches, bring up the needle, and trim threads. This will get the threads out of sight and the buried thread tails will either be quilted over with subsequent quilting or become entangled in the batting fibers.

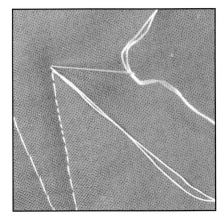

IMPORTANCE OF DOODLING

Doodling on paper is actually a very relaxing and fun way to start free-motion quilting. It is also a very important part of the process because it teaches you to see where a design needs to flow from one area to the next and how to get from one path to another. Doodling a specific design and repeating it many times on paper increases your confidence when you finally start quilting on fabric. It also gives you a chance to come up with your own design.

99% of my designs are freehand. I will quilt around designs that are part of the fabric, or quilt around an appliqué, but I always add my own stitches to fill around them or fill in the negative space.

I rarely use stencils, and I certainly don't discourage anyone from using them. If uniformity is important to your quilt design, stencils may be very helpful. Remember, they can be modified at all times, adding pebbles or other motifs to add interest. Then the quilting becomes more of your own design.

2¢ My Two Cents

Following-the-line-quilting (free-motion, and not walking foot) involves quilting according to a set design, whether it is custom or from a stencil. This technique is actually more difficult than you would think.

Precision is important in following-the-line quilting. And that means skill is required to move your quilt sandwich just right to navigate a curl, a curve or whatever is on the design. Hopefully, your muscle memory has improved, making it easier to accomplish this technique. Doodle the design on paper or practice quilting a set design on a practice sandwich. Whatever you do, it's always a good idea to step back and practice, practice, practice!

Thread Talk
FROM MY SEWING MACHINE

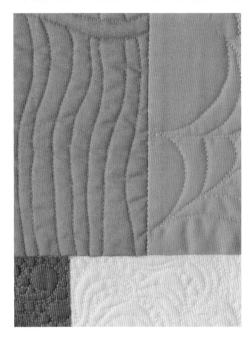

2¢ My Two Cents

Trying something new can be scary and daunting! However, my experience in machine quilting is that once you get over the learning curve, it will happen more easily. But you will need to be determined to get over that initial hump. I always start with echoing. If you are able to echo shapes at a somewhat equal distance apart, you will have a good feel for how to move your quilt sandwich. Many other designs and techniques are actually extensions of echoing, creating fancier renditions.

BRAIN POWER

Besides getting the muscle memory in your arms to register, it is also essential to get your brain on board so that you won't get tripped up by "where do I go" during the quilting process.

ONE WAY TO PRACTICE

When I teach beginning machine quilting to students, I exercise "tough love" and have my students echo around a shape at a distance of about 1/4" from the edge of the shape. Once they get the hang of moving the quilt

sandwich with the feed dogs disengaged, we keep echoing around the shape.

When students start out, they will probably experience uneven and jerky stitches echoed around the shape. As they go around and around with the echoing, they will gradually feel more comfortable and relaxed. Soon, the echoes will look less jerky and smoother in appearance. I have

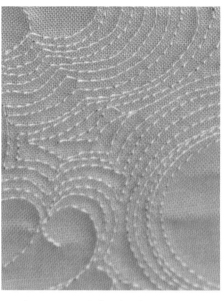

to admit it is a hard exercise, especially for beginners. But what the exercise does for them is to immediately get used to moving the quilt sandwich and building muscle memory.

As a challenge, after basic echoing is mastered, I ask quilters to keep quilting the echoes closer and closer together. It zooms in on the muscle memory to help move the quilt sandwich for an even tighter effect.

Echoing will lend confidence to quilting other motifs like swirls, and feathers. Amazing quilting results don't have to use complicated quilting motifs. Sometimes one basic motif (like a swirl, echoing, or even pebbles) can produce an equally stunning visual result!

ACHIEVING EVEN QUILTING

The visual perception of evenness in your quilting plays an important role particularly in an allover quilting design. It gives the viewer a sense of continuity and uniformity.

The challenge in achieving even allover quilting comes from the quilter being limited to only seeing the area under the throat of the machine at any given time in the process.

TIP

MY ADVICE FOR ACHIEVING EVENNESS:

- *Doodle your quilting motif or design on paper at roughly the same size or scale you plan to quilt on the quilt. That gives you an idea how many repetitions of the motif you will be able to quilt in the allotted space. Knowing your motif well before you actually quilt it will save you a lot of frustration.*

- *Start by training yourself to quilt even echoes. I mentioned the importance of mastering echoing before tackling anything else. Quilting echoes trains the quilter to master moving the quilt sandwich, as well as training the eye to gauge distance. If you haven't tried this before, refer to page 30 and practice quilting echoes roughly 1/4" apart until you feel comfortable gauging distance. Being able to visually gauge the spacing between motifs when quilting will automatically make your quilting more even.*

- *Spread your quilt out on the floor from time to time. See if you've missed any areas or quilted more loosely in one area than the rest of the quilt.*

Thread Talk
FROM MY SEWING MACHINE

2¢ My Two Cents

There are times when I will print out an image of my quilt top and start thinking about how I might quilt it well before I get to the actual quilting process.

If trying to eyeball distance between echoes is too overwhelming, it is perfectly okay to mark the echoes on the fabric! I have had students start out this way.

Sometimes I overlay a plastic sheet on the quilt top and doodle quilting designs that I think might work on the quilt with an erasable marker. That keeps me from having to actually quilt on the quilt to see the effect during the brainstorming process.

Thread Talk
FROM MY SEWING MACHINE

QUILT DENSITY

Quilting density has to do with the spacing between quilting motifs. Your spacing can be tight or loose, as long as the overall scheme is evenly spaced. It will give the viewer a visual sense of a well-quilted quilt.

The general evenness in distance around motifs is what gives your quilting a uniform look. Evenly spaced quilting gives the eye a sense of continuity and doesn't draw attention to one particular spot on the quilt. As long as there are no gaping holes that scream "quilt me!" you should be okay. Don't be afraid to go back and fill in areas that seem to need additional quilting.

DETERMINING WHAT AND WHERE TO QUILT

When I am ready to start quilting a new project, these general principles help me decide what to quilt.

- If the quilt top has busy prints, I generally go with an allover quilting pattern. This will give it a nice quilted texture without competing with the fabric. Otherwise, your lovely custom quilting could get lost in the busy fabric design.

- Is there an appliqué motif or element that can easily be converted into a quilting motif? Looking for clues in the fabric prints can help you choose a quilting design. If a motif is large enough, I might quilt on them directly. If not, I can use the pattern in the fabric as a starting point for an allover quilting pattern.

- If most of the fabric in the quilt top is solid or tone-on-tone, I tend to quilt more densely. The quilting becomes the star and will show up much better on the fabric.

- The general theme of a quilt also gives helpful clues. For example, if it is a Christmas quilt, I would quilt a holly and swirls motif

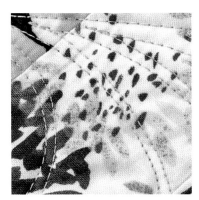

PRINTS

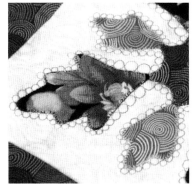

APPLIQUÉ

CLUES

SOLID

QUILTING NEGATIVE SPACE

Negative space is the large expanse of background area in a quilt. Using it for quilting can result in a very striking visual. Many contemporary or modern quilts adopt this design principle. Quilting in negative space can utilize a planned quilting scheme, or unplanned doodle-quilting of various motifs.

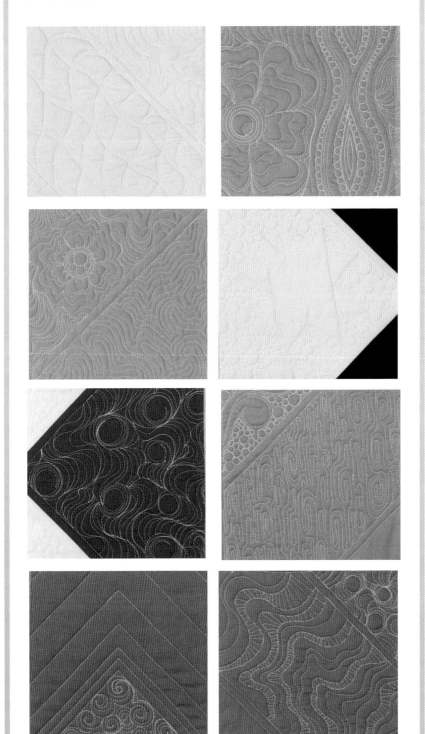

Thread Talk
FROM MY SEWING MACHINE

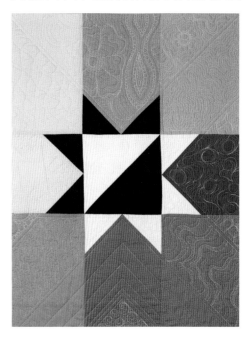

2¢ My Two Cents

PLANNED QUILTING...

is determined before beginning to quilt by marking the design on the quilt top. You will know exactly where to quilt what. It can be any combination of straight and free-motion quilting.

UNPLANNED QUILTING...

is "go with the flow" quilting. For example, you may quilt random straight lines all over a quilt or use free-motion quilting to add a variety of motifs over a large area of negative space. With no pre-planning of designs, your quilt becomes an empty canvas to fill with beautiful quilting!

Thread Talk

FROM MY SEWING MACHINE

2¢ My Two Cents

There are times when it is best to let the "block geometry" of the block determine your quilting plan. I had planned to quilt feathers on this quilt, but I decided the spinning pinwheel blocks needed to feel airy and light. I tried out a few ideas on paper first before deciding on the quilting design.

As it turned out, I used quilting to give the blocks more movement. I quilted a curve along the long sides of the "blades" and then echoed once. Then I filled the area around the pinwheel with fillers like tendrils, and swirls.

QUILTING APPLIQUÉ SHAPES

The easiest way to quilt appliqué motifs is to echo around the shape.

Quilt directly on the appliqué pieces to enhance them.

You could choose an overall design and quilt over the appliqué shapes as well.

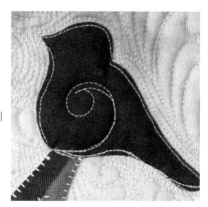

Instead of using a straight stitch, try quilting pebbles as an echoing pass around the appliqué pieces.

Another option would be to create a design in the background or negative space to make the appliqué motif pop out from the surface of the quilt.

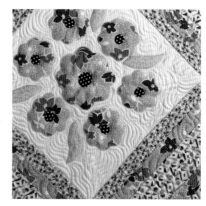

ALLOVER QUILTING

Allover quilting is not bound by the geometry of the block or the layout of the quilt. The same pattern is repeated over and over on a quilt top.

Prepping is incredibly important for allover quilting. Basting is a must to avoid puckers and pleats on the back of your quilt. I press and starch my quilt top before basting, especially when I plan to do an allover design, and I pin baste using LOTS of pins.

You want your pattern to be the same size and density, as close as possible, across the entire quilt. It's very important that you practice and know the motif well so you can avoid stumbles and being caught off guard, not knowing where to go next.

Take breaks and look back over what you have already quilted. I often stop and step back to see if there are any areas that need more fill, and then go back and add in more quilting. There is no shame in having to go back over areas you've already quilted.

Remember to square up your quilt after quilting an allover design. Manipulating your quilt sandwich under and through the throat area of your machine can stretch or shift the fabric. Squaring up your quilt before binding is good practice no matter what method of quilting you choose to do.

Thread Talk
FROM MY SEWING MACHINE

My Two Cents

BACKGROUND QUILTING

To make the main motif or shape stand out on a quilt top, background quilting will typically be smaller in scale. In the quilt above, I quilted the negative space around the feathers with a scale as small as I could manage. This really made my feathers pop.

It is not always necessary to quilt every bit of your quilt. Hopefully, with the tips shared here, you will be able to have a better idea on what to quilt, and what to leave unquilted on your quilts. Remember, the more you do it, the better your quilting becomes.

Thread Talk
FROM MY SEWING MACHINE

2¢ My Two Cents

QUILTING A BORDERLESS QUILT

Quilting borderless quilts presents a different set of challenges. You don't have the guideline of a border to rely on when it comes time to square up your quilt.

Before you start to quilt, trim the batting and backing even with the quilt top. Baste around the edge with a loose machine zigzag stitch to keep the quilt from becoming wonky as you quilt.

TIP

QUILTING A BORDERLESS QUILT

TIPS FOR QUILTING A BORDERLESS QUILT USING A DOMESTIC MACHINE:

- *Using batiks or other high quality fabric with a higher thread count will help maintain the squareness of a quilt. If your fabric feels like it has a looser weave, be sure to use plenty of starch while cutting and piecing, and square-up more often as you construct the quilt top.*

- *Use a lightweight batting for easy maneuvering. I use cotton batting instead of silk batting when my quilt is borderless.*

- *Choose a simple quilting scheme that doesn't require you to pull and scrunch your quilt in all possible directions while quilting it. This will help alleviate distortion issues as well. Simple grid-quilting along the major straight lines of the quilt works really well.*

- *Use slightly longer stitches when quilting in the ditch on borderless quilts. I find this causes less puckering in my quilt sandwich, and it preserves the squareness of the quilt.*

- *If your quilt happens to get distorted in the quilting process you can wet your quilt to tweak, pull and re-shape the squareness of the quilt. But try some of my other suggestions first. It might help you avoid this step.*

STRAIGHT LINE QUILTING

I prefer the even, clean look of stitches when I straight-line quilt. To maintain this look when I'm using my walking foot, I use an Accents in Design Fine Line Quilting Ruler.

The key to using the ruler is to butt it against the quilting foot and anchor it with your hand. Apply constant pressure and maintain the same grip through an entire quilting pass. Lots of concentration is needed! After finishing the first pass, take a deep breath and a break before attempting the next.

I recommend sticking with the smaller rulers for quilting on your domestic machine, like a 6″ or 8″ ruler. I find the smaller rulers easier to handle.

The ruler has scored markings so you don't have to mark your quilting lines. But I mark my quilts anyway. I find that moving the quilt, moving the ruler AND checking my quilting pass against the scored lined is too much to do at one time. Practice using the ruler to find out which method works best for you.

The Fine Line Ruler isn't as useful for quilting in the ditch because your seam may not be perfectly straight, especially if the surrounding area is already quilted. If I have to quilt in the ditch during free-motion quilting to move from one spot to the next, I simply free-motion that straight line. The stitches should "bury" themselves in the "ditch" and not be visible.

Thread Talk
FROM MY SEWING MACHINE

My Two Cents

STRAIGHT LINE OR FREE-MOTION

I typically use my walking foot to quilt straight lines. Even after learning to free-motion quilt, I will change to my walking foot and engage the feed dogs to quilt any straight lines. I like the line of stitching to be even and clean. I don't quite get that look when I am free-motion quilting.

My Two Cents
THE STITCH VARIATIONS

Echoes 30
Loops 31
Reflections 32
Sand Dunes 33
Swirls 34
Swirly Tails 36
Swirly Vines 38
Swirly Flowers 40
Embellished Swirly Vines 42
Easy Swirl Flower 44
Jester's Hat 46
Twirly Whirly 48
Pebble Power 50
Nifty Little S's 52
Cross-Hatching 53
Feather Plumes 55
Doodling Feathers 58
Feather Wreath 60
Roundabout Feathers 62
Sashing Feathers 64
Pseudo Feathers 66
Combinations 67
Designing with Simple Shapes . . . 68
Practicing Stitch Variations 71
Developing a Quilting Style 74
Quilting within Patches 77

LEARNING TO STITCH ----------------------------------

In this section, I share with you step-by-step directions to learn and practice the stitches I often use. Learning stitch designs is similar to when you learned to write; you practice the individual letters (stitches) over and over until you feel comfortable with them, then you start to combine the letters to form words (stitch designs or motifs). The practice can be done on a practice sandwich, or with a pen or pencil on paper.

Each stitch design is broken down into easy steps with a starting and stopping point for each step, and arrows to give the direction to stitch. The consecutive stitches are illustrated in a different color to make your stitching paths easier to follow.

For each step, the section you are stitching is shown as a solid line with arrows. The previously stitched sections are shown as dashed lines. This will make it easier for you to focus exactly on the part you are stitching.

A finished stitch sample is photographed on each page so you can see the effect of the finished stitch on fabric in one thread color. No two quilters stitch the same so don't worry if your stitches don't exactly match the illustrations. Keep practicing!

1 Disengage the feed dogs and carefully stitch around the shape of your motif. At each dot, stop and take a breath. Move the sandwich in the next direction following the arrows.

ECHOES

Echoing a shape or motif is the best practice for a beginner to gain control and fluidity. When first mastering echo quilting, slow down your stitching. This will help with the quality of your stitches more than anything else.

I encourage my beginning students to try echo stitching approximately 1/4" between passes and work to quilt the echoes closer when they are comfortable with the motif. Echoing is a background effect—it's okay if the echoes aren't spaced exactly.

If you are having trouble getting the hang of it, practice drawing. You can also mark the echoes on the fabric if you need extra help. Echo to your satisfaction on paper before trying it on your quilt sandwich. This is a good way to get in the "groove" with any design.

> Trace the illustration with your finger or a stiletto to get the "feel" of the motion for the motif.

2 Stitch your Echoes as close as you can possibly manage. When you have made one full round, continue stitching the next Echo.

3 Remember, Echoing is a background effect – it's okay when the echoes aren't spaced exactly.

LOOPS

Practicing Loops is a great way to loosen up, especially for beginning quilters. It is a very forgiving motif that can be used as an allover pattern in sashing and for borders.

Try adding in other motifs between Loops such as stars, hearts, or flowers, or go around your Loops twice for a different effect.

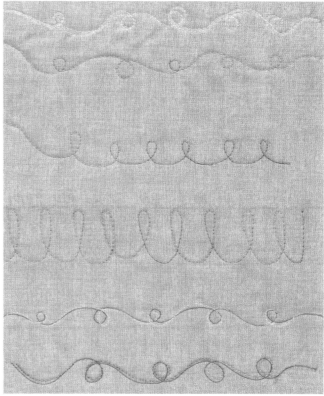

1 This design is simply a meandering line with Loops added. Learning this stitch will make it easier for you to do any meander stitch and to stitch pebbles (page 50). To use this as an allover design, change directions at the dots to wind around in random directions.

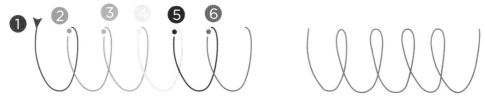

2 These stitches are similar to making lowercase e's and l's in handwriting. I have my students practice both of these to loosen up their arms and shoulders. The familiar penmanship shapes come natural to us because we learned to make them long ago with a pencil and paper.

3 For a fun border effect, try quilting a second line of Loops over the first, using a contrasting color of thread. This gives a "shadow work" effect that hand embroiderers use.

REFLECTIONS

This stitch combines straight line free-motion quilting with a meander design that looks like ripples or reflections in a pool of water.

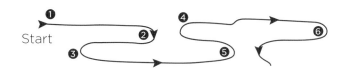

1 Stitch a horizontal line with a half-circle turn, stitch a parallel line about half the length of the first line, turn again and continue stitching to the next dot.

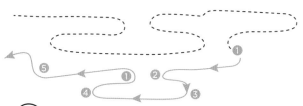

2 Continue turning and stitching as shown by the blue path.

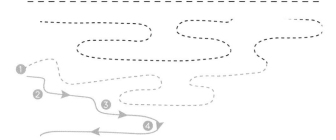

3 At the dot, stop, take a breath, then continue stitching the green path in the direction of the arrows.

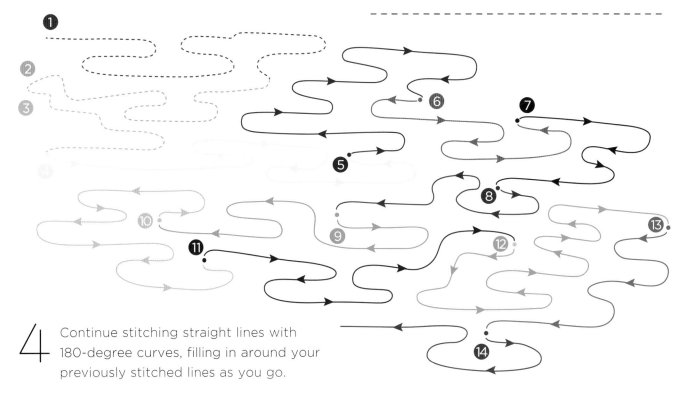

4 Continue stitching straight lines with 180-degree curves, filling in around your previously stitched lines as you go.

Start

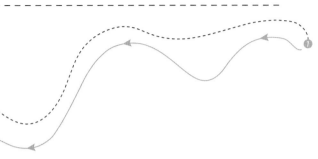

1 From starting point, quilt a loose wavy line in your quilting area.

2 Turn and quilt a second wavy line along the first line.

3 Repeat at opposite end, continuing to make wavy lines to fill your quilting area. I like to combine other stitches with the wavy lines, such as the back and forth loops shown here, for variety and interest.

Trace the illustration with your finger or a stiletto to get the "feel" of the motion for the motif.

SAND DUNES

Sand Dunes are like echoing without having to follow any rules with echoes that are not equally spaced. Here I added back and forth lines between two Sand Dune passes for a railroad track motif.

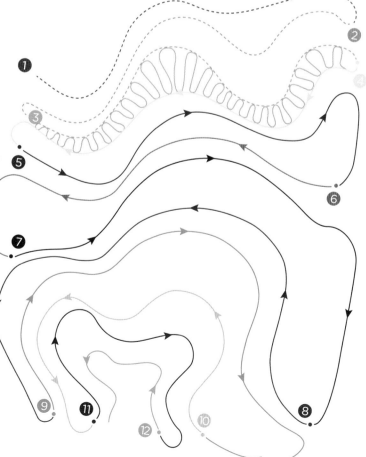

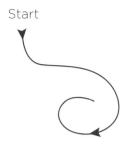

Start

1   Start with a soft s-curve that curls in on itself.

SWIRLS

This is a design that works best after practicing on paper for awhile. Doodling the design will help you understand how to move from one area to the next. I often use driving for quilting illustrations. When I navigate a curve on the road, I slow down so I don't run off the road. It's the same with quilting. Slowing your stitching down is the key to mastering curves. When your stitching speed is reduced your stitches will be smaller, so your curves will naturally appear smoother.

Keeping your Swirls evenly spaced creates a pleasing visual effect. But, don't be afraid to experiment with slightly uneven spacing.

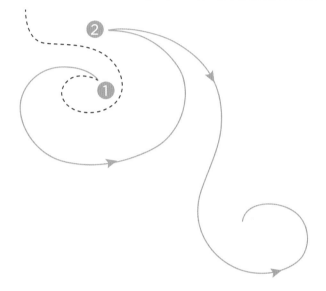

2   At the dot, stop, take a breath and change directions. Echo the first curve, forming a hook. Stop at the dot, change directions and create a second, longer s-curve.

3   At the third breathing point, change directions again and echo the last curve creating a hook.

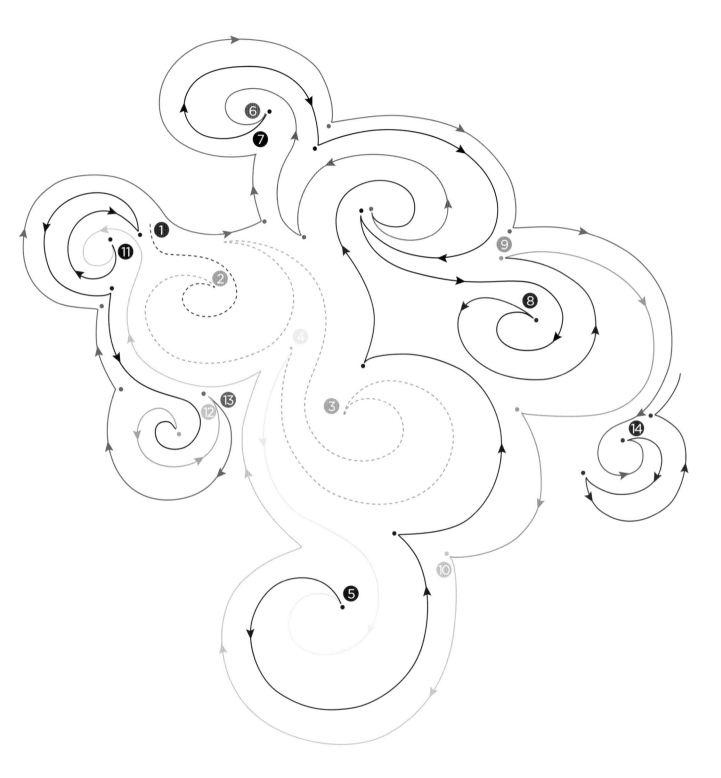

4 Continue echoing and adding s-curves to fill in around your stitching.

SWIRLY TAILS

This stitch variation is similar to Swirls on page 34, but with a leaf shape, or "tail" added to the end of your swirls. After making the pointed "tail", your next connecting line should be a soft curve to maintain the flow of the allover motif.

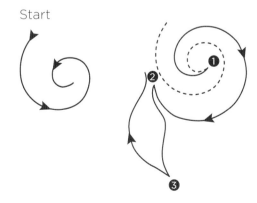

Start

1 Stitch a c-curve. At the dot change directions to echo the first curve. At the next dot, stitch a shorter wavy line, pause at the dot and add a second wavy line to create a tail.

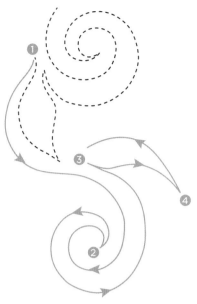

2 Stitch an s-curve along the tail as shown in the diagram. At the dot, echo that curve until you are close to the edge of the inner swirl. Reverse directions tightly and add a tail at the end.

3 Stitch another s-curve and echo stitch the curve.

If your space is limited or you need to fill a gap, stitch a small tail, echo the curve again then stitch a larger tail at the end (3) & (4).

4 Continue adding swirls and tails as needed to fill the space, adjusting the scale and direction of your curves as needed.

When doodling, you might practice drawing on paper exactly how the stitch path is shown. That might give you an idea on how to better navigate directional changes when quilting the repeats of a quilting motif.

SWIRLY VINES

This is a design that definitely benefits from practicing first on paper. Notice in these schematics how one swirl cluster moves to the next. I move my swirls back and forth in various directions to fill up the space. There is not much regularity with this motif. You go wherever you want, adding your swirls and tendrils to fill the quilting area as needed. The key is to keep the stitching evenly distributed. This is one of my all-time favorite quilting designs.

Start

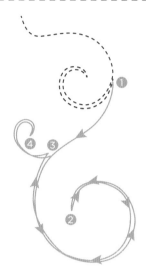

1 Stitch a swirl at the first dot. Change direction and backstitch to the next dot.

2 From the first dot, stitch a second curve. Restitch along the same path of the curve and add a small curl to the vine.

3 From the first dot, stitch a long curved line with a loop. Reverse directions and stitch back over the loop down to the vine (3). In the opposite direction stitch a small curl (4). Add a large curve and finish at the vine again.

4 Continue adding vines and loops as needed to fill the space, adjusting the scale and direction of your curves as needed.

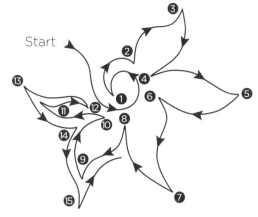

SWIRLY FLOWERS

This stitch variation with pointed flower petals looks great on holiday quilts or any traditional quilt as an all-over quilting design. The pointed petals are a little more "elegant" than typical rounded flower petals.

Trace the illustration with your finger or a stiletto to get the "feel" of the motion for the motif.

When changing directions you can stitch forward, backward, or side-to-side and never have to turn your project.

1 Start with a swirl. At dot 1, pause, reverse directions and echo the swirl a short distance, change directions and stitch a wavy line to start forming the first petal. From dot 3, change directions and stitch a second wavy line to form the first pointed "petal". Repeat this to create 4 more petals. From dot 12 change directions and echo the previous two petals.

2 Begin the second swirly flower with a swirl. At dot 2 reverse directions and echo the swirl. Change directions at dot 3 and stitch a wavy line to start forming the first pointed "petal". Change directions and stitch a second wavy line to finish the first petal. Repeat this to create 4 more petals. From dot 12 change directions and echo the last petal.

3 Continue adding swirly flowers as needed to fill the space, adjusting the scale and direction of your petals as needed.

EMBELLISHED SWIRLY VINES

You will want to master the basics first before moving on. In this case, the "basics" is the Swirly Vines stitch (page 38). Don't try a stitch like this before becoming comfortable stitching the curves and arrangement of the basic stitch first.

Embellished Swirly Vines simply add a short series of petal lobes at the base of the swirl before you start another swirl. To get out of a corner, echo around the lobes to get to a space where you can start another swirl.

Start

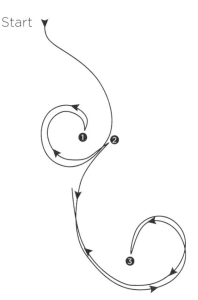

1 Start with a swirl. At the dot, pause, reverse directions and trace the path back to the middle of the curve. Pause again, change directions and stitch a larger swirl facing the opposite direction. Pause at the tip, then retrace the stitching path back down the vine.

2 Pause at the dot, take a breath and stitch a gently rounded "hook" shape, pause, reverse direction and stitch a second, third, fourth and fifth petal, pausing briefly at each dot.

3 Continue stitching, adding vines and petals to fill your quilting area.

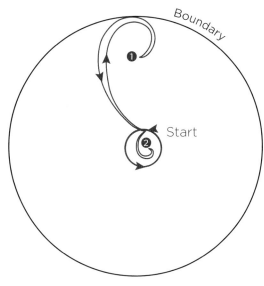

EASY SWIRL FLOWER

This is easier than it looks; it just takes some practice to create designs within a boundary. As you can see in my stitch sample above, the swirls do not all have to be identical to look good and the echoes do not have to be exactly spaced. Once you echo quilt around the swirls you will form the flower petals and no one will notice if the flower isn't perfect. You can echo just one time around, or multiple times like I did. This motif works well if you are quilting within a block.

2 Stitch the small circle, then add a tiny swirl inside this circle. At the tip, reverse directions and retrace your stitching path back to the small circle. Stitch a larger swirl that extends to the boundary. Reverse directions and trace this swirl back to the base.

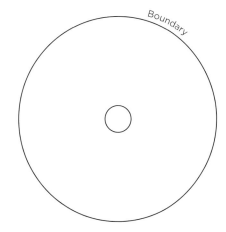

1 Use a marking pen or pencil to draw a circle as the outer boundary for your flower. Draw a smaller circle in the center for the inner boundary.

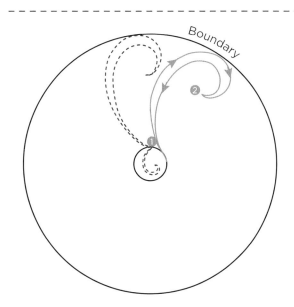

3 Stitch a second large swirl the same size, retracing the stitching path back to the base of the swirl.

To quilt this stitch all over a quilt, try stitching multiple flowers randomly scattering on a quilt top. Then fill in the background (negative space) with background quilting like pebbles.

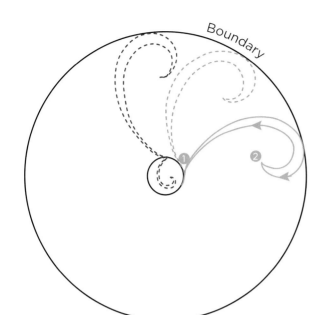

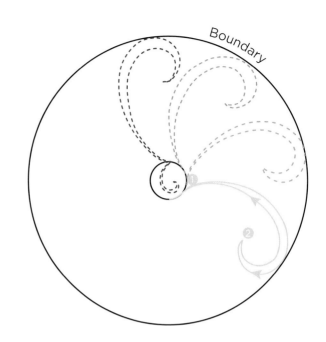

4 Continue adding swirls, keeping the size the same and spacing them apart at roughly the same distance.

5 Don't worry if your swirls don't look exactly the same, this will improve with practice.

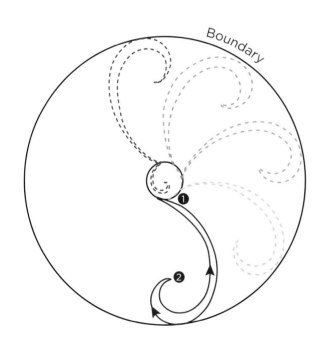

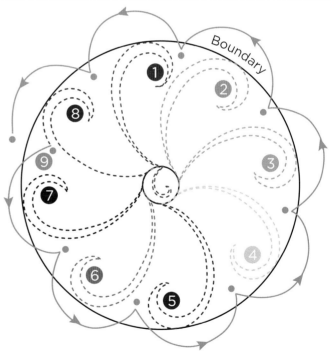

6 Continue stitching adding swirls to fill the circle.

7 On last swirl, pause at the tip, reverse directions to stitch back down the swirl, but stop about one third of the way. Pause, and change directions to echo the swirl tips to create flower "petals". You can echo around the motif as many times as you like.

JESTER'S HAT

The key in quilting this design is to NEVER echo more than one swirl at a time. Instead, quilt another hat "point" to move around the area. This design is very fun and casual when applied as an allover quilting motif.

If you try this design and struggle with it at first, try enlarging the scale of it. Quilting your "hats" at 2.5" - 3" wide will make them much easier to stitch than tiny 1" hats.

> Trace the illustration with your finger or a stiletto to get the "feel" of the motion for the motif.

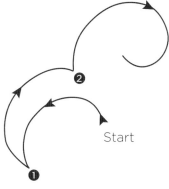

1 Stitch a concave arc, and at the dot, pause, take a breath and echo the arc to make the first point of your "hat". Pause again at the dot, then stitch a swirl.

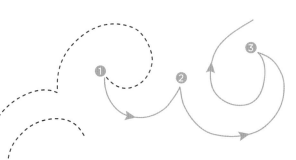

2 At the dot, start to echo the swirl, creating a convex arc. Pause at the dot and stitch a c-curve. Change directions and stitch a swirl inside the last curve.

3 Pause at the dot, change directions and stitch a swirl. Pause again, take a breath and echo the swirl, creating a convex arc Pause again, stitch a swirl and echo that swirl as shown.

4   Continue stitching echoed swirls, and arcs to fill in the area. You will notice your stitched swirls start to look like a jester's hat.

TWIRLY WHIRLY

This is a fun, easy motif that works great as an allover design on quilts for kids and simple quilts. You are basically quilting loops (see page 31) and triangle shapes.

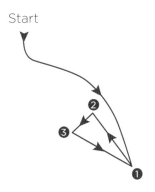

Start

1 Stitch a wavy line, pause at the end, and stitch an elongated triangle. Pause at each point of the triangle to take a breath and change direction. Return to the end of your wavy line to complete the triangle.

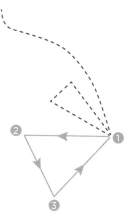

2 Stitch a larger triangle next to the first triangle, remembering to pause and change direction at the dots.

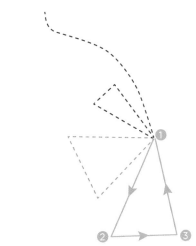

3 Continue stitching straight lines to form triangles.

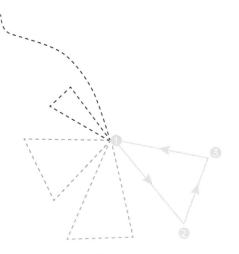

4 Stitch triangles of various sizes around the center point.

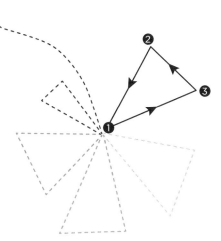

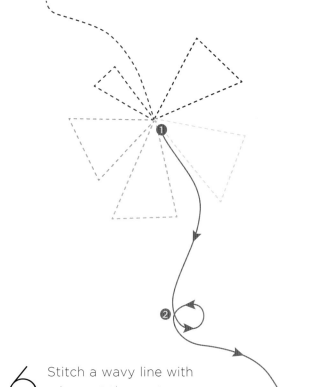

5 Stitch a fifth and final triangle to finish the whirly. Stop at the center dot.

6 Stitch a wavy line with a loop at the center.

7 Continue adding whirlys (triangles) and twirlys (loops) to fill in around your original stitches and fill the area.

By the same token, you could replace triangles with teardrops for a fun floral variation.

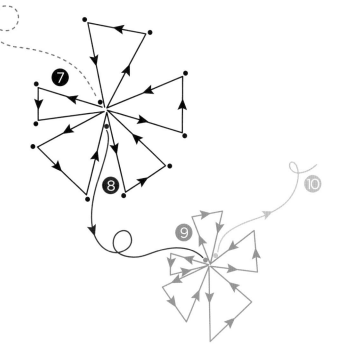

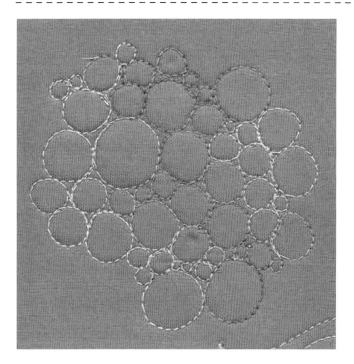

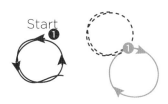

PEBBLE POWER

Pebble quilting is comprised of circles of different sizes and is a great way to practice stitching curves and circles. The various sizes make it easy to hide the not-so-perfect circles. It creates a beautiful texture around other quilted designs, such as feathers, or it can stand on its own.

I quilt a complete circle and then backtrack on part of the circle to go to the next spot where I want to start a second circle. The process is repeated again and again until an area is filled with circles.

Pebbles are my favorite to quilt for background quilting because they are so forgiving. Sometimes the pebbles don't end up exactly round, but they in no way diminish the visual effect.

Start

1 Start by stitching a circle anywhere within your area to be quilted. Stitch around the circle twice, pause, then stitch a second adjoining circle, or pebble.

2 Stitch a third circle that connects to both the first and second circle.

3 As you complete each circle, continue around that circle to get your needle to the point where you want to start your next circle. Stitch another adjoining circle.

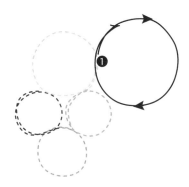

4 Continue adding circles, or pebbles, remembering to vary the sizes.

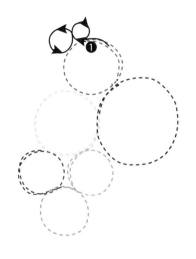

5 Add circles around the previously stitched pebbles.

6 Continue adding circles of various sizes, creating a cluster of pebbles.

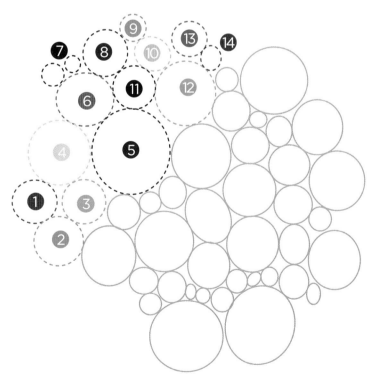

7 As you fill up the area, you can use smaller circles to fill in the gap between bigger circles.

8 Continue stitching pebbles to fill your quilting area.

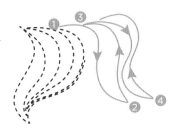

I often stitch over previous stitches to get to unquilted areas—don't worry if you have to do that.

NIFTY LITTLE S's

First I make an elongated "S", then I repeat the S's to make a nice little stack of 4-5 S's. Once a stack starts to look monotonous, I change the direction of my stitching and start a new stack.

As you can see in the bottom right corner of the sample above, this stitch can be combined with others, such as Pebbles, or used as a filler around Feather Quilting.

2 Stitch a wavy line, or S, pause at the dot, and stitch a second wavy line. Repeat two more times.

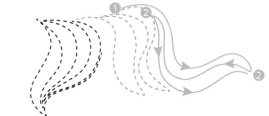

3 Continue to change directions and vary your stacks. This is a forgiving design and nothing needs to be exact.

4 Vary the length and shape of your stacks to fill a space.

5 Longer S's can be used to create a space to fill in or travel around previous stitching.

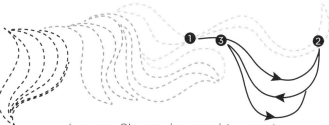

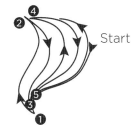

1 Start by stitching an elongated "S". At the dot reverse directions and stitch a second S. Repeat three more times. Retrace the stitching path to get to a point where you want to start your next S set.

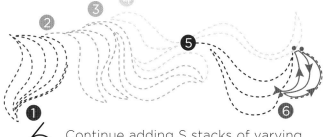

6 Continue adding S stacks of varying sizes to fill your quilting area.

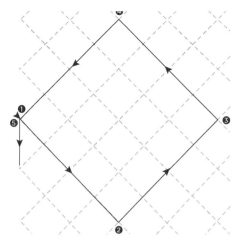

1 Start by stitching a square with one corner along the edge of the quilting area.

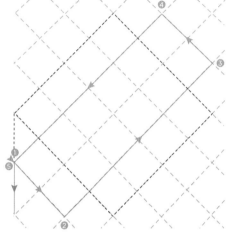

2 Travel by stitching down to the next line along the edge of the quilting area, then stitching a rectangular shape.

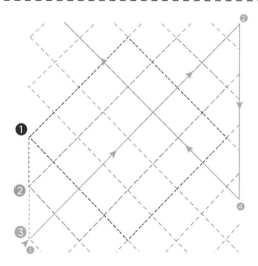

3 Again, travel down along the edge of the quilting area to the next line, Continue stitching rectangles and triangles until you stitch over all of your drawn lines.

CROSS-HATCHING

Cross-hatching works well as background quilting and as allover quilting. Cross-hatch quilting over appliqué pieces can create a soothing, blended look.

A few tips for cross-hatching:

- Make sure your lines are marked as accurately as possible for maximum visual effect. Time invested in marking is always time well spent.

- I use my walking foot to cross-hatch because I prefer the uniformity of the lines.

- I recommend wool or silk batting for dense cross-hatching because the individual diamonds really POP! However, when cross-hatching far apart, I prefer to use a cotton blend (80/20) because, to me, it gives a cleaner look than the wool or silk.

- Use the needle-down function on your machine.

- I starch my quilt top before I baste when I know it will be cross-hatched, and then pin baste close together.

Thread Talk
FROM MY SEWING MACHINE

2¢ My Two Cents

How your feather lobes look determine the appearance of the entire feather plume. It is definitely a worthwhile investment of your time to sit down and draw out how best to execute the curved lobes. Some quilters prefer slender, even lobes, while others prefer the lobes to be a bit more full. I like them both ways and try to incorporate slender and full lobes when I can. Knowing what you are looking for in your own feathers is the first step in beautiful feather quilting.

ANATOMY OF A WELL-FORMED FEATHER PLUME

- Smooth curvature as you round the feather lobes.

- The width of the feather lobes should decrease as the curvature approaches the spine.

- Make sure the smoothness persists to end where the feather lobe meets the spine.

- I backtrack along my previous feather lobe to get to the point where I want to start a new lobe. I find that the new lobe looks more substantial that way.

- I work on my feathers one side at a time. This gives me better control of how my feathers turn out.

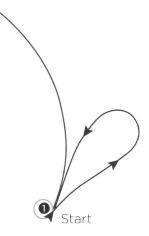

Start

1 Using a marking pen or pencil, draw a curved line where your feather spine will be. Starting at the bottom of the line, stitch a gently curved teardrop shape for your first lobe.

FEATHER PLUMES

My tricks for achieving free-motion curvy, feather plumes:

- I start stitching at normal speed, until I come to and slow down at the entrance to a curve, similar to slowing down and turning into a curve while driving.

- I mentally divide the curve into four quadrants, and try to keep the number of feathers somewhat even from quadrant to quadrant.

- When I need to orient the feathers in a different direction than my feather started with, my lobes become much shorter. This is the key to turning your feathers along a curved spine!

When changing directions you can stitch forward, backward, or side-to-side and never have to turn your project.

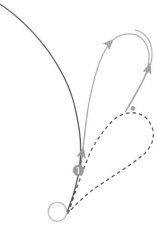

2 Reverse directions, and stitch a second lobe, continuing the curve back to where it meets the first lobe. Stop at the dot, reverse directions and backtrack about halfway along the second lobe.

3 Pause at the dot, take a breath, change directions and stitch a third feather lobe.

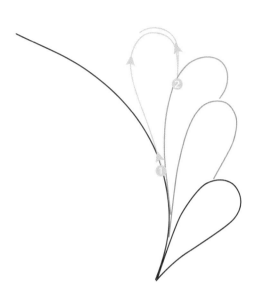

4 Continue adding lobes and backtracking along the previous lobe to get to where you want to start the next one.

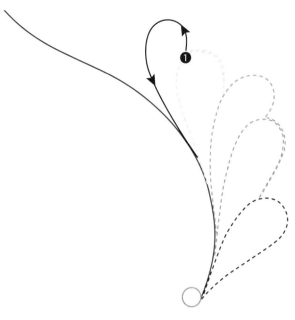

5 I vary the length and width of my individual lobes for variety and interest, as shown here. If you prefer even sized lobes, use the same stitching path but practice making your lobes even and uniform.

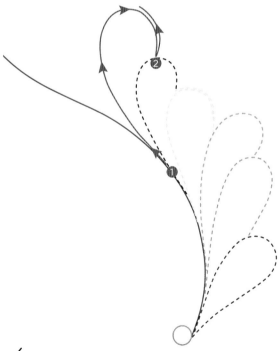

6 Stitch along the spine, preparing to turn into the curve of the next feather lobe. Stitch to where it meets the previous lobe, pause, take a breath, reverse directions and backtrack to where you will start the next lobe.

7 Continue adding lobes along this side until you get to the top of your spine.

8

After you finish the lobes along one side of the feather spine, either knot, cut and bury your threads, or retrace your stitching down the spine to get to the base.

Begin adding lobes to the other side in the same manner. To follow the inside curve of a feather spine, you will need to shorten and narrow your lobes to fit within the curve.

DOODLING FEATHERS

I have had this little secret for years and now I'm going to share it with you! This is what I call my dandy way of doodling feathers for beginners.

Use this doodling technique to practice feather lobe formations. Before I could free-hand quilt my feathers I drew out my feathers this way, then transferred and marked them on my quilt tops. Then I quilted them by following the lines.

Once you are familiar with the doodling, you can vary the feather lobes by drawing them outside of the leaf outline boundary. It will give a bit more "flow" to you feather plumes.

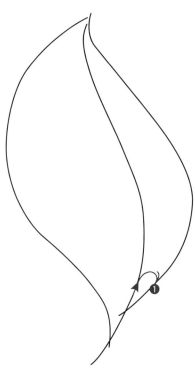

1. Imagine the feather plume to be like a leaf. Begin by drawing the spine and leaf outline. Using a marking pen or pencil, draw a curved line where your feather spine will be. Starting at the bottom of the line, stitch a gently curved teardrop shape for your first lobe.

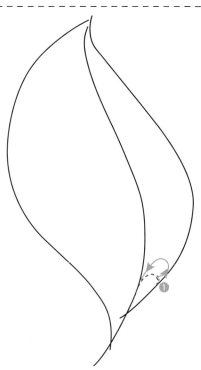

2. Reverse directions, and stitch a second lobe, continuing the curve back to where it meets the first lobe. Stop at the dot, reverse directions and backtrack about halfway along the second lobe.

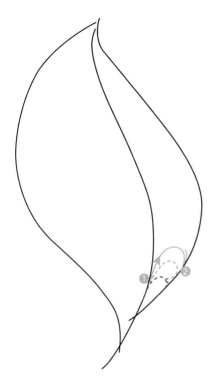

3 Continue adding lobes, backtracking along your path of stitching as needed to get to the next starting point.

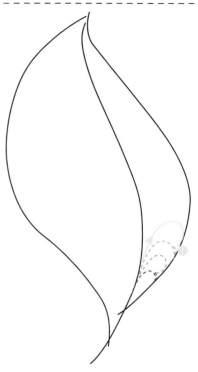

4 As you continue adding lobes, remember to pause at the dots, take a breath, and think about where your needle will move next.

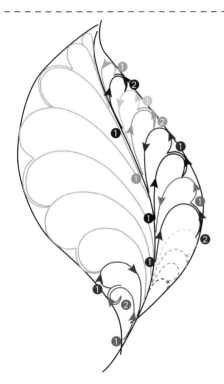

5 Continue adding lobes to fill the entire leaf outline.

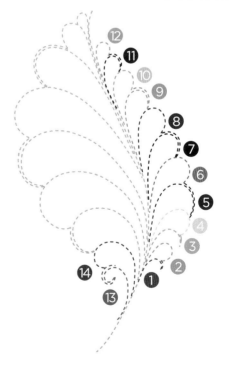

6 Once you have filled in the entire leaf, erase the leaf outline and you'll see the feather plume shaped like a leaf.

FEATHER WREATH

As I start stitching a wreath, I only "half-form" the first feather. The reason is I don't know how well my last feather will match up with the first feather once I am completely around the wreath. Not fully forming the first feather allows me room to "adjust" the first and last feathers for the wreath lobes to fit as nice as possible.

Note: Feathers can be quilted going in either direction! Combining them in different directions will create an interesting visual effect.

Experiment with the sizes and styles of your feather lobes to achieve different looks.

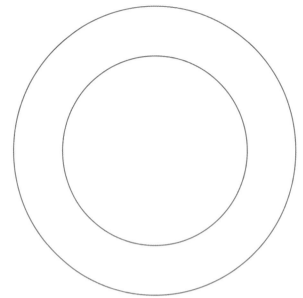

1 Using a marking pen or pencil, mark the inner and outer perimeters as shown.

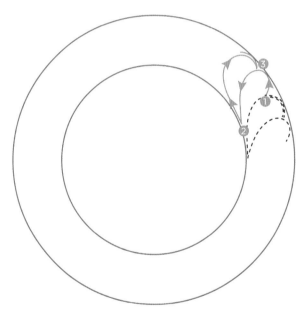

2 Start near the outer ring, forming a half-feather lobe by stitching a c-curve. Pause at the dot, take a breath and stitch a second lobe as shown. Backtrack along your stitching path to where you will start your next lobe.

Stitch the next lobe, being careful to make your lobes as close to the same size as possible. Pause at the dot, reverse directions and stitch another lobe. Backtrack along the top of this lobe to where you will start the next one.

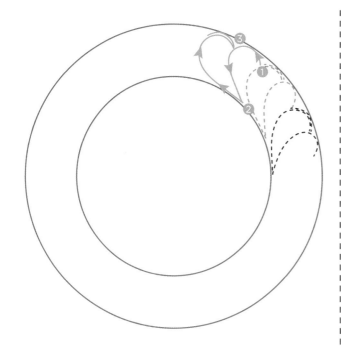

3 Continue adding lobes, backtracking along your path of stitching as needed to get to the next starting point.

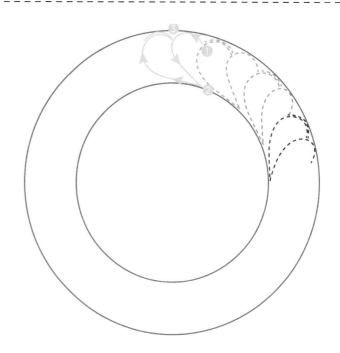

4 As you continue adding lobes, remember to pause at the dots to take a breath, and think about where your needle will move next.

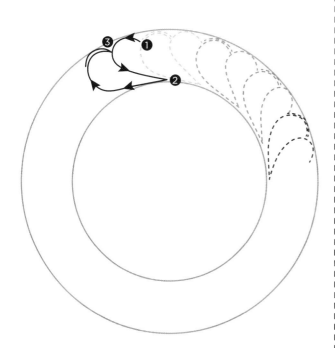

5 Pausing at the dots, and consciously taking breaths will keep you from tensing up as you focus on creating "perfect" wreath lobes.

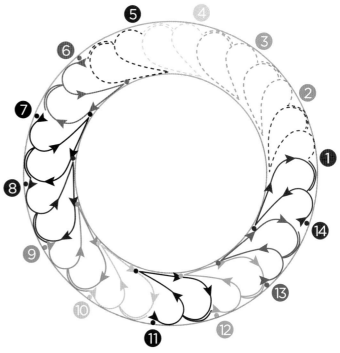

6 Continue all the way around the wreath, and notice your final lobe closes the first, half-formed lobe you stitched. If necessary, you can adjust the width of your last few lobes to fill the gap if it isn't coming out nice and even.

ROUNDABOUT FEATHERS

These feathers are free-hand quilted with very minimal marking. I mark two circles on the space I want to fill. The inside circle forms the spines of feathers. Roundabout Feathers are very versatile. I can place them wherever I want within an open space, vary the ring sizes and spine placement, and combine with filler stitches to further customize their appearance. Note: Feathers can be quilted going in either direction! Combining them in different directions will create an interesting visual effect.

The key is to remember the inside feathers of the inner ring MIRROR the outside feathers of the outer ring.

1 First, mark two circles using a marking pen or pencil.

2 Start near the outer ring, forming a half-feather lobe by stitching a c-curve. Pause at the dot, take a breath and stitch a second lobe as shown. Backtrack along your stitching path to where you will start your next lobe.

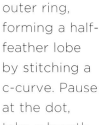

3 Stitch the next lobe, being careful to make your lobes as close to the same size as possible. Pause at the dot, reverse directions and stitch another lobe. Backtrack along the top of this lobe to where you will start the next one. I vary the length and girth of my lobes to add interest and create the effect of overlapping feathers.

4 Continue all the way around the wreath, and notice your final lobe closes the first half-formed lobe you stitched. If necessary, you can adjust the width of your last few lobes to fill the gap if it isn't coming out nice and even.

5 Start near the inner ring, forming a half-feather lobe by stitching a c-curve. Pause at the dot, take a breath and stitch a second lobe as shown. Backtrack along your stitching path to where you will start your next lobe.

6 Stitch the next lobe, being careful to make your lobes as close to the same size as possible. Pause at the dot, reverse directions and stitch another lobe. Backtrack along the top of this lobe to where you will start the next one. I vary the length and girth of my lobes to add interest and create the effect of overlapping feathers.

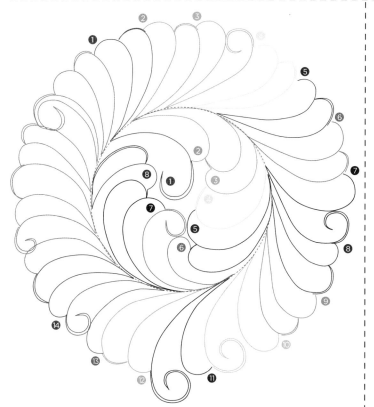

7 Continue all the way around the inner wreath to fill the circle.

Try setting the inner circle off center for a different effect. Just remember to mirror the inside feathers to the outside feathers and you'll have a beautiful Roundabout Feather.

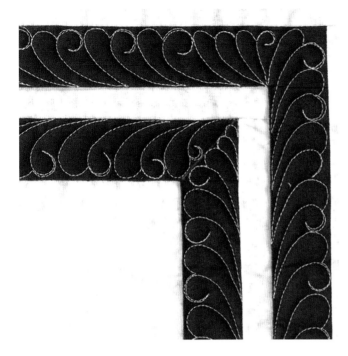

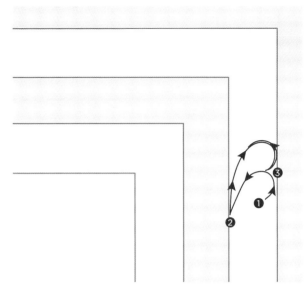

SASHING FEATHERS

It is also possible to quilt feathers in sashing. You would treat the outer edge of the block, or prior sashing/border as your "feather spine". This is a free-hand exercise. You will want to be comfortable with the stitching path of feathers before trying this variation. Feathering a rectangular sashing all around is a variation of the feather wreath (page 60).

It can be hard to decide what to quilt on sashing. Feathers can really dress it up!

1 Using the seam lines between blocks and sashing as your guides, start by forming a half-feather lobe by stitching a c-curve. Pause at the dot, take a breath and stitch a second lobe as shown. Backtrack along your stitching path to where you will start your next lobe.

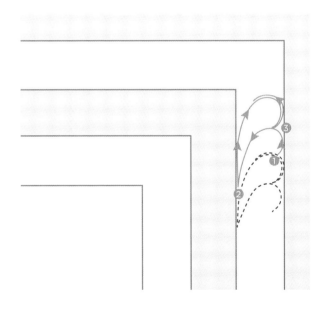

2 Stitch the next lobe, being careful to make your lobes close to the same size. Pause at the dot, reverse directions and stitch another lobe. Backtrack along the top of this lobe to where you will start the next one.

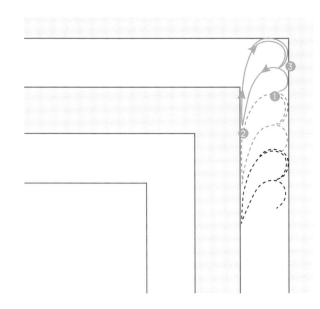

3 When you come to a corner, if your lobes are facing outward, you will just slightly turn your lobes to fit the corner as shown. If your lobes are facing inward, you will need to miter your corner as shown in Step 5.

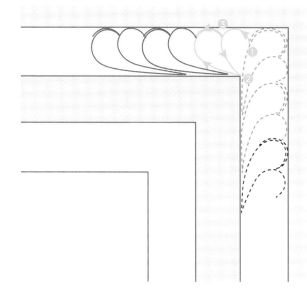

4 Continue around the sashing, adjusting lobes at the corner as needed, until you come to the last lobe, which will close the first, half-formed lobe you stitched. If necessary, you can adjust the first and last lobes to fill the gap.

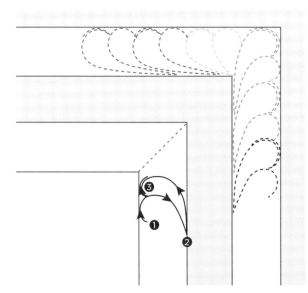

5 Start stitching the inner sashing by making a C-curve facing the opposite direction. When you come to a corner, mark the 45-degree line as shown. Decrease the size of your lobes to fill in the 45-degree area.

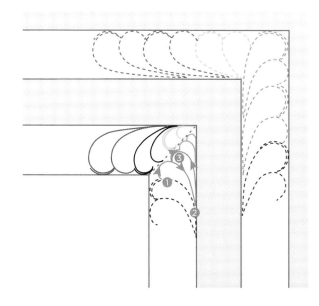

6 On the other side of the 45-degree line, start with a small lobe, and gradually increase lobes to full size. Continue all the way around the wreath, closing the last and first lobe by adjusting as needed.

PSEUDO FEATHERS

These Pseudo Feathers are more forgiving and much easier to quilt, and I think they provide the perfect opportunity to practice the rounded curvature in the midst of the quilting process. The basic idea is to form a feather lobe (solid line), and after the rounded curvature is formed, echo closely along the previously stitched path (dotted line) to return to the spine before forming the next lobe.

You will notice that not all are perfect, but as a whole, the feathers look smooth and uniform. The goal is to form the lobes with a curvature as gracefully round as possible.

The stitch sample above shows a few more variations. In the center are two "leafy" variations where the lobes stand apart as individual leaves. This variation works well as a quick border motif. On the left is an echoed feather plume stitched the same way as the plume in the schematic. On the right, lobes are closed to make a formal feather.

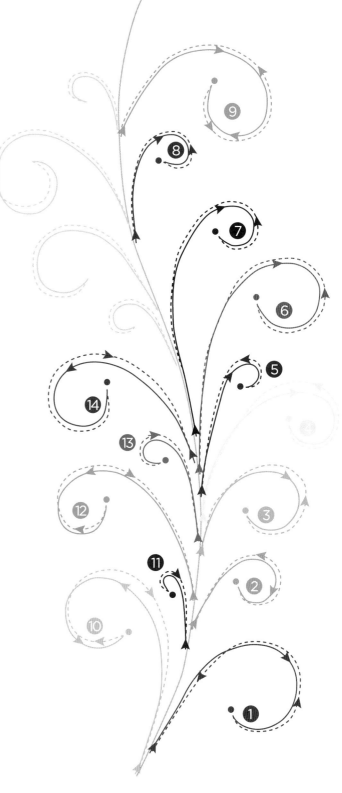

COMBINATIONS

I often combine echoing, pebbles, Nifty Little S's and feathers for a fancier presentation of background quilting.

Quilt panels are perfect for jumping right into free-motion quilting because they involve very little construction. I like that I can go right to basting the quilt sandwich and then proceed to the machine quilting process. It is an inexpensive way for beginners to practice on an actual project.

Following the Lines

Simple shapes allow me to quilt "following-the-lines" quilting. Following the lines is more of a challenge for me than just quilting wherever I want to go, but it's a great way to sharpen your quilting skills and practice quilting more accurately. Simple shapes also provide the opportunity for adding Echoing after following the lines.

You can see that I add my own touches along the way. For instance, I added different details on the flowers and filled in some of the crevices with background quilting.

In the grass area, I quilted Nifty Little S's, Echo stitching and Pebbles for the background quilting (see pages 52, 30 and 50).

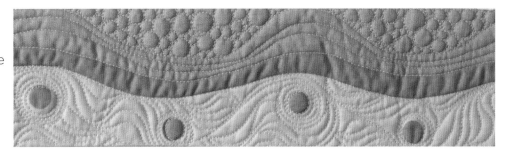

Designing with Simple Shapes ------------------

Background Quilting

Choose background quilting
stitches you want to practice. I
decided to use Swirly Vines for
this panel (see page 38).

Shapes With Room

Choosing a panel with simple shapes will allow you to try out different motifs like I did on the flower pots
and the Dresden sunshine on this panel.

Fabric Inspiration

When deciding what to quilt
on a quilt, you can often find
inspiration in the printed fabric.
For instance, the leaf on one of
the flowers in this panel inspired
a quilting motif I added to the
tree branch.

STITCH SAMPLER

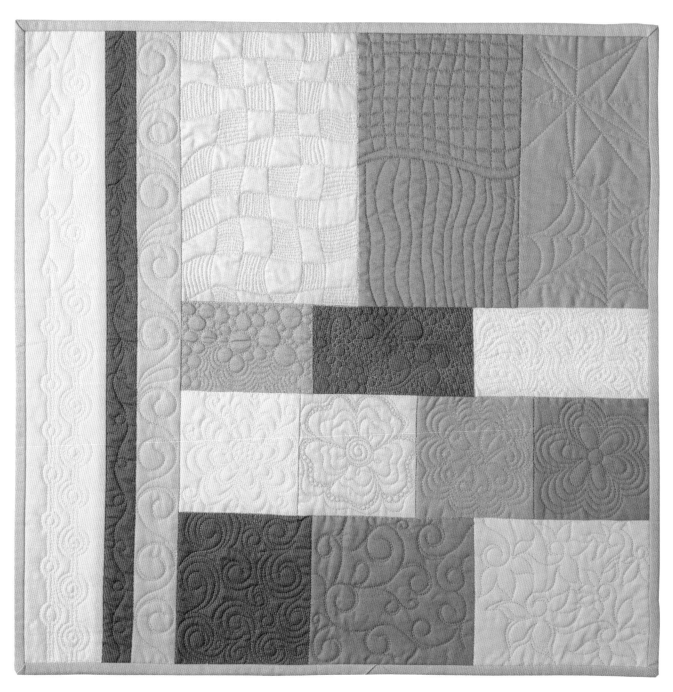

One of the things I love about machine quilting is how easy it is to build upon something simple to get new stitch variations. Once you get the basics down, the options are endless. I designed this Stitch Sampler and quilted it to demonstrate how you can build upon the basics,

Quilting Motifs

Section 1—

I use my walking foot to stitch-in-the-ditch before free-motion quilting. Swirls are an effective way to quilt borders and sashing. In the grey border I added a lobe embellishment in between each swirl. In the red border I added accents to a line of Loops. In the yellow border are variations of concentric circles and a heart garland.

Section 2—

In the lime rectangle I quilted back and forth lines inside the alternate squares of the Cross-hatching (see page 53). In the orange rectangle, I started by quilting wavy lines, then added perpendicular wavy lines for curved Cross-hatching. I used a walking foot in the blue rectangle to stitch 5 criss-crossed lines. I added more straight lines to create a star. Using curved lines instead gives me a spider web effect.

Quilting Motifs

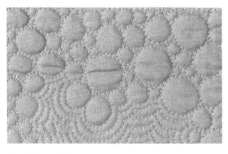 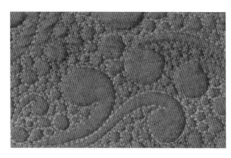 

Section 3—

In the blue area, I quilting Pebbles of various sizes, and echoed around the pebbles as a secondary motif. The red area shows the combination of Pebbles with a scroll shape (a variation of the basic Swirl), and finally in the yellow rectangle, Pebbles combined with Nifty Little S's. All 3 incorporate Pebble quilting but the look is completely different in each combination.

Section 4—

These four squares show different floral motifs that can be quilted to fit any square. The idea is that once you get a basic flower shape, accents may be added here and there (Pebbles, Swirls, Loops, etc.) to make your floral motif fancier. Play with the placement of your Echoes, or add Pebbles within two Echo stitched lines. The options really are endless.

 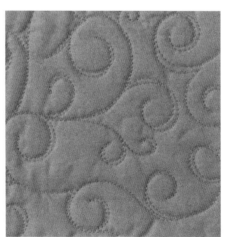 

Section 5—

Once you master quilting the basic Swirls (page 34), and can quilt them comfortably, you can have fun trying different variations of swirls. The red area is simply the basic Swirls (page 34), Swirly Vines (page 38) are shown in the orange area, and Swirly Flowers (page 40) are quilted in the lime rectangle.

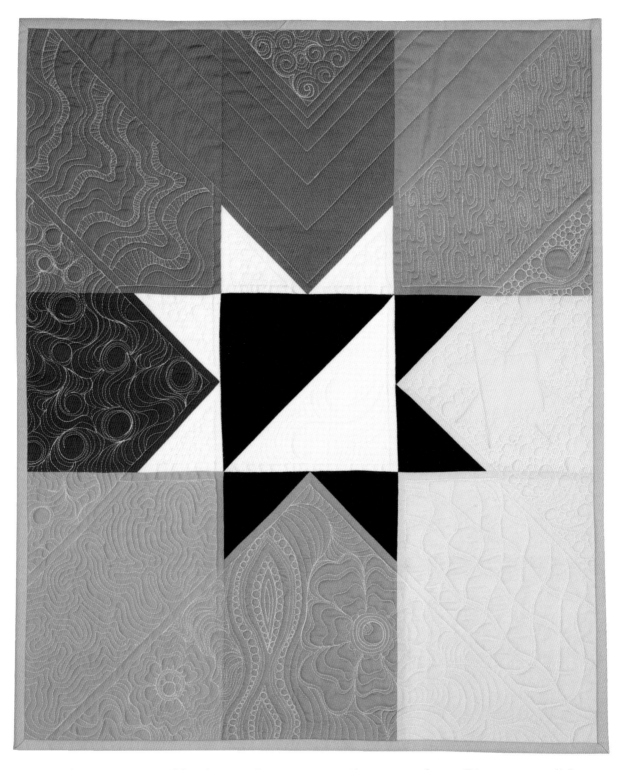

Leaving a large expanse of background area, or negative space, for quilting can result in very striking visual effects. Many contemporary or modern quilts utilize this design principle.

Instructions for assembling the Modern Star Sampler can be downloaded from:
http://landauerpub.com/uploads/file/mod_star_sampler.pdf

Quilting Motifs

Section 1—
I use my walking foot to quilt the straight line portion and fill in with Swirls on the area at the top of the V (see page 34).

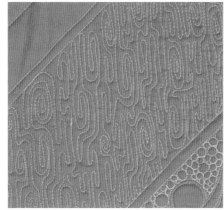

Section 2—
As a background filler, I used Reflections (see page 32).

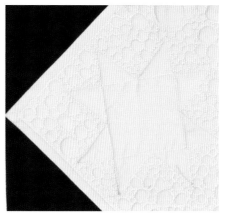

Section 3—
I used my walking foot to quilt a sawtooth star, then added Pebbles as a background filler (see page 50).

Section 4—
Double wavy lines are quilted close together in both directions to form a curved Cross-hatch variation. This is stitched the same way as regular Cross-hatching (see page 53).

Section 5—
I started by quilting the "eye" shape, Echoed it a few times, added some Pebbles, and free-motion flowers. Nifty Little S's were used as background filler (see page 52).

Section 6—
Start out as you would with stippling, then Echo stitch evenly around your stipples.

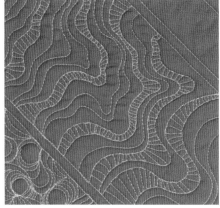

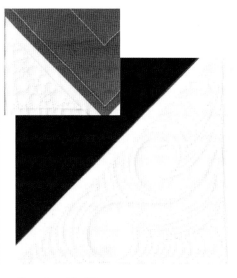

Section 7—
I quilted circles then closely echoed several times before adding Nifty Little S's to fill in around the circles (see page 52).

Section 8—
Sand Dunes were quilted with back and forth perpendicular lines for the railroad track effect (see page 33).

Sawtooth Star—
Pebbles fill the white star points and curved scroll shapes are Echo quilted to fill the large white triangle.

Marking

1. Mark 1/4" around the center sawtooth star. Extend the block geometry and mark lines to the edge of the quilt top, creating 8 distinct sections. Mark 1/4" within each section.

2. Mark "V" lines, varying the widths at 1-1/4", 1", 3/4", 1/2", and 1/4" in Section 1.

3. Mark a small Sawtooth Star in the middle section of the third block in Section 2.

4. Mark the perimeter 1/4" inside the white triangles.

Note: I prefer to do my marking before basting my quilt sandwich.

The quilt center is made of squares and rectangles of different colors. Use each rectangle to practice a different background design. I chose to have the Roundabout Feather plumes from the border "spill over" into the quilt center, but you could just quilt one stitch variation in each center patch to practice filling that specific area. The feathers spilling into the quilt center demonstrate that it's perfectly okay to quilt outside the box to add visual interest.

Instructions for assembling the Bird Wallhanging can be downloaded from:
http://landauerpub.com/uploads/file/bird_applique_wallhanging.pdf

Quilting Motifs

Yellow—Pebbles and allover Feathers
See pages 30 and 55.

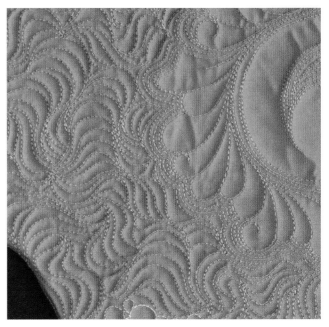

Copper—Nifty Little S's
See page 52.

Coral—Cross-hatching with Pebbles
Quilt the Cross-hatch first (see page 53), then fill alternate squares with Pebbles (see page 50). You could add any stitch in the alternate squares to practice different combinations.

Gray—Straight Line quilting
I use my walking foot for quilting straight lines most of the time. However, when the straight lines are quilted densely, as they are here, I would free-motion quilt them.

Wendy's Quilting Suggestions

For this wallhanging, I created two Roundabout Feathers as the origination point for the feather plumes. I always mark some before I quilt feathers. I use a water soluble fabric marker to mark the feather spines. The circles on the marking diagram below are the guidelines for my Roundabout Feathers, which I quilted first, then quilted the feather plumes. After I filled up the quilting area with feather lobes, I used Pebbles and Echo quilting as filler stitches. Densely quilted echoes made my feathers pop more than just the pebbles alone. If you are not comfortable free-handing the feathers, try marking out the lobes and quilt the feathers by following the line. That is how I started out quilting feathers.

Marking Feather Spines

DEDICATION

Dedicated to my husband, who has been there since the very beginning of my quilting journey;
as well as my 8-year old daughter, who has become my dearest stitching friend!

ACKNOWLEDGMENTS

- Barbara Herring—Barbara is my quilting teacher, mentor and friend. If Barbara had insisted that I made her usual beginner quilt that has four patch blocks, I probably wouldn't have progressed the way I have. Instead she patiently and graciously helped me through the design I had picked out (a pieced and appliqué design that is really meant for an early intermediate quilter) to make as my first quilt. Over the course of my quilting journey, she remains a constant encourager in my life!

- Rogers Sewing Center—The people at my quilting "mother ship" have been a great source of encouragement and support. I count Dan and Rhonda, of Rogers Sewing Center, two of the dearest people in my life.

- The Landauer group—This book would not have happened without the very capable editorial team at Landauer.

- My little family—I am appreciative of my husband who is more than supportive in all my quilting endeavors. Without his understanding, this book would not have happened. Despite his own busy schedule, he has offered countless times to do school run and take care of dinner while things got frantically crazy for me. Our daughter who keeps me on my toes. With her in my life, I am forced to better manage my time, ha!

- My parents—I owe my parents for all the adventures I have been able to have in my life. They raised me with the vision to do my best, and sustain me through their faithful prayers.

- Quilting Friends—Quilters are some of the sweet people on earth, and they definitely include the many quilters whom I have met online through my blog. In so many ways, this is their book too!

- My Lord and Savior, apart from Whom I am nothing. I seek to reflect His beauty and glory through my work, albeit a very feeble endeavor on my part. Soli Deo Gloria!

SPECIAL THANKS

Thankyou to the following companies for their generosity in helping me make my book projects happen

Auriful Threads

BERNINA of America

Hobbs Batting

MODA Fabrics

Genie Magic Bobbin Washers

Supreme Slider by Pat LaPierre

**Accents in Design Fine Line
Quilting Ruler**